This is a product of the world we live in.
That is why It has failed.
That is why It has succeeded.
The choice of perspective is THEIRS.

I am a product of the world I live in.
That is why I have failed.
That is why I have succeeded.
The choice of perspective is MINE.

You are a product of the world you live in.
That is why you have failed.
That is why you have succeeded.
The choice of perspective is YOURS.

We are a product of the world we live in.
That is why we have failed.
That is why we have succeeded.
The choice of perspective is OURS

Exordium

ETERNAL INIQUITY

ROMEO
RUSSELL
ARCHIBALD

12.21.2020

If your love exists in eternity, then die in it
Take this place with you
It was never yours, but it could be
Lay your life on the fertile ground you've scorched
Teach the world to never tread near a star

Forever Son

We reject the light
Our photic reflex when it's bright
Now it doesn't shine like it used to
Was there a sign from the clouds?
Strong winds brought a breeze far too cold
It's rained ever since
There's a rumor that you won't return
I've been counting the days
I thought we cycled like seasons
We need you
Nothing grows without the Son

This way?

Love you… This way?
We've never been here
I'm learning, let me try
I FUCK UP

Hold you… This way?
I'm uncomfortable and won't stay still
You get irritated and push me away
I LAY ALONE

Drive you… This way?
You're anxious because I suck at driving
Music plays to change your mood
I HEAR THE SILENCE

Feed you… This way?
It took me way too long to place your order
You don't have an appetite anymore
I FEEL STARVED

Hear you… This way?
I wanted to help you, not hurt you
Maybe I missed the message
I SHUT UP

Leave you… This way?
Yes, but I didn't go as myself
This doesn't feel right
I LOST SOMETHING

Redeem you… This way?
I'm better now, I can show you
This can work
I LOVE YOU

Abandon me… This way?
It broke me in every way
I healed, I learned so much
I THANK YOU

Sacrilegious Love

For every moment of clarity, there's an eternity of clouded judgment

Yours is always the first to pour rain

As waters rush, here I am, swimming upstream, sinking

Its the thought of you that continues to give me refuge

Lost and isolate, romanticization gives sight to salvation

The enigma of this loneliness fuels love's desperation

Helpless to each midnight, watching as every memory grows sweeter

You become more than a woman, and I transgress into less than a man

The goddess in my head is remorseful in love

The sanctuary that saved me is plentiful

But as my senses recover, I am reminded that this place is not a home... it's just a place

And this woman is not a goddess

The Nihilist
(Nietzsche's Theory)

As a child I told God that I would suffer all my life, if it meant the ones I loved wouldn't struggle throughout mine.

When I'm gone, hold them close.

Bring them into the divine.

Hand me the early death, though I never favored time.

Does that explain this pain, could those words be the reason?

Are we catalysts or cattle?

A burden or a beacon?

I never faltered patterns or sought to honor sequence.

I told you what was lost and shared with you my secrets.

Maybe all that's left is here, with no God to interfere.

Desperate for salvation as we pacify our fears.

Freedom preached through verses, yet here we are in chains.

Enslaved to the reality in which we create.

Contemplating break from monotonous confusion.

Could chaos be prescribed for this Earthly disillusion?

Penance for my vices in this desolated ruin.

See that I am freed.

Don't bind me to this fate.

Wheel of time, recycled life, existential change.

BLACK SHEEP

Running from my fate, I feel death isn't far

No time to rest, I can't tell them apart

As my eyes get heavy, I pray my feet don't fail me

If I succumb to my environment, I'm sure it will kill me

Everywhere I look there's people close to the edge

I block out the noise to hear the voice in my head

It says God is here, so I keep both eyes open

But nobody's been seen, and no message was spoken

Which form it appears, there's no way to tell

I tried searching for heaven but got lost in this hell

Sure, others got it worse, but tell me how should I feel?

We both share this life, what could my time reveal?

There's a whole lotta questions that no one can answer...

I'm sure somebody knows, but they hold knowledge for ransom

Whatever comes after life can't be much worse than this

Numbing our souls until we no longer exist

If every dollar is debt, and birth certificates stock

I guess I'll work till I'm dead and my debts paid off

To each one I owe, I'll leave it at this...

FUCK THE WORLD TILL IM FREE

I DON'T OWE Y'ALL SHIT

No Tears

If you could feel me, then would you shed tears too?

Running thru insanity as I try to survive in this place
where I was born to die

Would you keep low... or get as high as you can?

I'm not asking you to understand, I just wanted to know
if you could feel.

But I don't see tears yet.

No tears for addicts, whose suffering is overpowered
by the sounds of their begging.
No tears for thieves, although they had nothing for
themselves.
No tears for hoes, girls whose minds were broken, and
bodies stolen.
No tears for thugs, boys left for dead on the same
street that caged them.

The older generations lived fast, but we live faster.

Kids raised on pain create more kids, spreading
ourselves thin, until we can no longer see ourselves in
what we've created

So, keep on going

Keep medicating because your sick
Keep abusing because your damaged
Keep fucking because no one loved you
Keep killing over money because you lived without it

This crash course ends in natural disaster

So maybe it's in our nature to die by what we're after

But tell me... if all I wanted to do was live, do you think
they would kill me because of it?

Would they shed tears then?

The prayer,

If there's no heaven, could you share your paradise with those I've left behind.

They don't ask for much.

It's hard to imagine things you've never had.

I know times weren't always bad.

I just thought that happiness was too beautiful to be seen from a distance.

If they were there, I know they'd be peaceful.

Just enough to see them smile.

Enough to feel again.

The plead.

If there's no God, will you please hear their prayers.

Show them a life worth living.

Something we all could be.

My time has come, but with you there's hope.

There's nothing more I can do, but with you there's a chance.

Save a space for them.

Even if there's no room for me.

12:12

You invested what you refused to feel inside of me.

Buried deeply, into places that would take me years to uncover.

A young boy, experiencing the pain you mindlessly numbed.

I suffered as a consequence.

Suffering that bled into everything I touched.

That damage began to perpetuate cycles.

Cycles I spent years lost within.

Years even I can't find.

I lost my faith in you, God, and myself.

I lived within that shame and guilt for a long time.

I hated who I'd become.

Hate which festered into a deep pain.

Pain that I refused to feel.

I turned my back on everything I loved.

With no direction, I continued to descend into myself.

ETERNAL

As seen throughout history

The abandonment of god

The enticement of mystery

A return to the source

Though escape was great

As resulted in force

We all meet our fate

Souls which were lost

And those that are found

A life dreamt from heaven

Which ends in the ground

INIQUITY

Simply, we are vessels of energy, and a beacon to those which exist without. What lives beyond us is a reflection of ourselves. It is also apparent that we manifest from that same energy which we are birthed.

What is a creator without creation?
What is creation without a creator?

It is this duality which makes us inherent of flaw. What separates us from god is the abandonment of our own nature. We have been stripped of ourselves.

A void which may be filled. Error which awaits resolve. Wounds which would heal.

It is this potential of change that makes us as powerful as God.

Can we not breathe life into worlds?
Don't we kill them just quickly?
Can we still imagine, think, and create?
Would it all end if our mind drew blank?

Until you realize your internal cycle, life will always have a beginning and end.

How can God love what you reject?

This is our Eternal Iniquity

12:12

Unaware of my reality, I was blind to the changes that started to take shape.

The more I became aware, the more I began to see.

What I hated most about the world was found inside of my own being.

I was a reflection of everything around me.

With no path to follow, I continued to look within

My intuition led me to any tool I could find that would help me understand.

With each step toward knowledge of self, the universe began to become visible to me.

Information that I could not understand started to appear constantly.

Numbers frequently appeared in sequences, as affirmation of what I was experiencing.

Reoccurring events were no longer seen as random coincidences.

Paradoxical patterns seemed to live everywhere.

Each of us, cycling within our own nature, projecting life onto the world.

Cycles which have no beginning.

Cycles which have no end.

God's Son

I relinquish power from everything over me one
hundred times over

For all those lost, whose lives were cost, my
persistence moves forward

Though victory seems far, time apart, every day comes
closer

Despite this Hell, Hue-man spirit collected in cells, we
break free from flesh

Transmutation within phases of life

To comprehend darkness by finding our light

We live through suffering and die in desire

Somewhere between our spirit moves higher

Before this, there was nothing, so nothing shall remain

The death of all pleasure that's born from our pain

The Thought – The Creation

The thought of being free can overwhelm
ambitious minds

What can one discover beyond how they identify?

Afterthoughts of action, changes left unrealized

If nature's force is entropic course, what's left for us to
decide?

Is difference felt as we leave ourselves?

Are we creatures of habit, or something else?

Some label sin, without or within, but most is undefined

To serve the question, answered with perspective,
projected onto life

True knowledge comes freely,
but at what cost?

Nothing to be gained without something to be lost

Once gone away, let nothing remain

Bare heart and soul, mind broke from frame

Only then, reborn again

Us

Let this be your sign,

For every night that you died
Lying there awake
Curdled into yourself as you cried.

Let this be your love,

When it felt like you couldn't
Rejection settling in
You're worth diminishing as the mirror fed you lies.

Let this be your strength,

When everything came crumbling
After nothing was left
There you were.

Let this be our place,

So, we can build
You can always call it a home
I will never leave.

Let this be us.

A place of peace (Mine)

One day I will live forever
Inside the memories of those I've loved
That is the place I shall burrow myself
Though time may pass, know I will never die
Every tear a testimony to the pain we endured
A smile as you recall the beauty inside our moments
Somewhere that death cannot reach
Beyond life itself
That is where I'll be

17/5

Nature's hymn

The birds sing songs of a blue sky, flying so fast, with no place to land.

No flowers in sight.

I offer my hand as a home.

They learned to stop running long ago.

Now, I eagerly await their message.

As kind as a stranger, they return with stories of the day.

No time stands between us.

We are as unfamiliar as the day we met.

Their tongue is of another tune.

The ears before mine stopped listening.

Still, I wait, hoping one day to hear again.

Again, they visit, wishing the same.

It seems as though that's the only thing left to do now.

I wonder if everything before was a waste.

Maybe this is all there ever was.

The Roses

Remember where we're from
Everything we grow is a product of that

Displaced in concrete
Nowhere else to go

Some will see the way we live
Most won't understand

Uprooted from our land
Growing with no ground to stand

They bleed when the rose's thorns prick them
Yet proceed to pick them

Maybe we're the same way
Flowers begging to grow

In our nature to be beautiful
Sharing love as we're shown

Cut from our roots
Never given a chance to bloom

Our trauma stemming from that pain

And as we wither away, on display in their vase, we're
reminded that beauty dies

Maybe it's in our last breath, just like the rose, that we
return to God

We find ourselves there, decomposing, in the same
mud that birthed us

So, remember where we're from
Everything we grow is a product of that

You

Enamored by the beauty of the flower, they never
noticed you were born of dirt

Even though I knew

They never poured love

Not knowing time could grow life

You did not bloom just to wither away

I will always make sure you're loved

I'll always save a space for you

Even when they don't

Breaking the cycle of those who never noticed that
beauty was born of dirt

Denouement

What I am will fade

A man   A memory   An idea

All things eventually do

Just as silence finds space between the noise of life

Or skies returning rain to the ocean from which it came

This is the same

The moment I live inside lasted a lifetime

But in the end, it was only a moment

All I was

A man   A memory   An idea

Was just that

Take all that I offer

Receive no more than what you can carry

These words are only words

{Afterthought}

To my community, there's nothing I wouldn't give to save you.

In my 20 years, I spent most of my time convinced that you would be the death of me.

It took a long time to realize that you were the one thing giving me life.

In a world filled with so much ugly, I understand why it's hard to feel beautiful.

Even I am guilty of shaming you.

My wish is that this is seen as a sign of hope.

To anyone who will search, you will find pieces of me in this work.

I pray you discover parts of yourself.

Although, no matter how hard I tried, I feel incomplete.

So, I dedicate this to every boy and girl fallen from God.

My hope is that you will feel our connection and finish this story.

Love where you're from, it's a reflection of yourself.

You are our answer to **Iniquity**.

frē

/free/

1. no longer confined or imprisoned

2. to act as one wishes; not under control

3. not determined by anything beyond its own nature

fre collective LLC

Instagram: @frecollective |
Email: thefrecollective@gmail.com

Made in the USA
Middletown, DE
28 March 2022